Senior Moments

SENIOR MOMENTS

This edition copyright © Summersdale Publishers Ltd, 2019

First published in 2015 as *The Little Book of Senior Moments*

All rights reserved.

An Hachette UK Company
www.hachette.co.uk

Summersdale Publishers Ltd
Part of Octopus Publishing Group Limited
Carmelite House
50 Victoria Embankment
LONDON
EC4Y 0DZ
UK

www.summersdale.com

Printed and bound in Malta

ISBN: 978-1-78685-806-1

Senior
Moments

Freddie Green

summersdale

To...

From.................................

Inside every older person is a younger person – wondering what the hell happened.

CORA HARVEY ARMSTRONG

“

I can still enjoy sex at 74.
I live at 75, so it's no distance.

BOB MONKHOUSE

”

WHEN YOU DECIDE AGAINST BUYING YOUR LITTLE GRANDSON A JIGSAW PUZZLE LABELLED 6–8 YEARS. AFTER ALL, THEY ONLY HAVE A COUPLE OF WEEKS OFF SCHOOL AT CHRISTMAS.

Eventually you will reach a point
when you stop lying about your
age and start bragging about it.

WILL ROGERS

Every morning, like clockwork, at 6 a.m., I pee. Unfortunately, I don't wake up till 7.

ANONYMOUS

WHEN YOU CAN'T
WORK OUT HOW
THE CEREAL GOT
INTO THE FRIDGE,
AND START TO
FEEL NERVOUS
ABOUT WHERE
YOU MIGHT FIND
THE MILK.

"

Three things happen when you get to my age. First your memory starts to go... I've forgotten the other two.

DENIS HEALEY

"

WHEN YOU SEARCH HIGH
AND LOW FOR YOUR CAR
KEYS ONLY TO FIND THEM
IN THE CAR DOOR.

WHEN YOU'RE NOT TOO SURPRISED BY THE ARRIVAL OF A NEW FINANCIAL CRISIS – YOUR HAIRLINE HAS ALREADY BEEN IN RECESSION FOR 20 YEARS!

My doctor told me to do
something that puts me out
of breath, so I've taken up
smoking again.

JO BRAND

"

I have the body of an
18-year-old. I keep
it in the fridge.

"

SPIKE MILLIGAN

WHEN YOU RING YOUR FRIEND TO ASK THEM FOR THEIR PHONE NUMBER.

WHEN YOU INSIST ON HANDING OUT NAME BADGES AT ALL FAMILY GATHERINGS, ESPECIALLY SUNDAY LUNCH WITH YOUR SPOUSE AND CHILDREN.

As for me, except for
an occasional heart attack,
I feel as young as I ever did.

ROBERT BENCHLEY

“

I don't want to retire. I'm not
that good at crossword puzzles.

NORMAN MAILER

”

Men chase golf balls when they're too old to chase anything else.

As the talk turns to old age,
I say I am 49 plus VAT.

LIONEL BLAIR

WHEN YOU FIND YOURSELF
MARVELLING AT YOUR
CAR'S ABILITY TO MOVE
ITSELF FROM WHERE
YOU PARKED IT.

WHEN YOU'VE
BEEN ON HOLD
FOR SO LONG
THAT YOU'VE
FORGOTTEN
WHAT YOU
CALLED FOR.

"

I'm officially middle-aged.
I don't need drugs... I can
get the same effect just by
standing up real fast.

JONATHAN KATZ

"

You know you are getting older
when "happy hour" is a nap.

GARY KRISTOFFERSON

WHEN YOU STOP ON THE STAIRCASE TO CATCH YOUR BREATH, AND CAN'T REMEMBER WHETHER YOU WERE GOING UP OR DOWN.

WHEN YOU ARE BARRED FROM YOUR LOCAL SUPERMARKET FOR CAUSING CHECKOUT HOLD-UPS AS YOU TRY TO REMEMBER YOUR PIN.

Be kind to your kids; they'll be choosing your nursing home.

ANONYMOUS

INTERVIEWER:
To what do you attribute your advanced age?

MALCOLM SARGENT:
Well, I suppose I must attribute it to the fact that I have not died.

> My grandmother's 90.
> She's dating. He's 93.
> They never argue.
> They can't hear each other.

CATHY LADMAN

"

First, you forget names...
Next, you forget to pull your
zipper up and finally you
forget to pull it down.

LEO ROSENBERG

"

WHEN YOU
ANSWER THE
PHONE, ONLY
TO DISCOVER IT
WASN'T YOUR
PHONE THAT WAS
RINGING – IT
WAS ON THE TV.

WHEN YOU REALIZE THAT'S
FACE CREAM YOU'RE
SPREADING ON YOUR
TOAST, NOT BUTTER.

Do not worry about avoiding temptation. As you grow older it will avoid you.

JOEY ADAMS

"

I can still cut the mustard...
I just need help opening the jar!

ANONYMOUS

"

WHEN YOU FIND
THE PRESENCE OF
PUBLIC TOILET
FACILITIES
WORRYINGLY
COMFORTING.

Sex in the sixties is great,
but improves if you pull over
to the side of the road.

JOHNNY CARSON

WHEN YOU ARE OVERWHELMED BY THE URGE TO GET HOME, GET SETTLED INTO YOUR TROUSERS WITH THE ELASTICATED WAIST AND GET THE CURTAINS CLOSED.

WHEN YOU ARE
ANNOYED BY
THE FACT THAT
YOUR ALL-IN-ONE
REMOTE CONTROL
WILL NOT OPEN
YOUR GARAGE
DOOR. THEN YOU
SEE IT'S YOUR
MOBILE PHONE.

Old age is like a plane
flying through a storm.
Once you are aboard there
is nothing you can do.

GOLDA MEIR

WHEN YOU WONDER FOR A GOOD 20 MINUTES WHY YOUR VACUUM CLEANER ISN'T WORKING, THEN FIND IT'S NOT EVEN PLUGGED IN.

Exercise daily.
Eat wisely.
Die anyway.

ANONYMOUS

"

Interviewer:
Can you remember any
of your past lives?

The Dalai Lama:
At my age I have a
problem remembering
what happened yesterday.

"

WHEN YOU USE THE PHRASE "THE ONE FROM THE TV" TO DESCRIBE WHAT YOU'RE LOOKING FOR IN THE SUPERMARKET.

WHEN YOU SPEND HALF AN HOUR SEARCHING FOR YOUR GLASSES, ONLY TO FIND THAT THEY WERE ON YOUR HEAD THE ENTIRE TIME.

Old people should not eat
health foods. They need all the
preservatives they can get.

ROBERT ORBEN

" Middle age is when it takes
you all night to do once what
once you used to do all night.

KENNY EVERETT "

I smoke 10 to 15 cigars a day; at my age I have to hold on to something.

GEORGE BURNS

When we're young we want to
change the world. When we're
old we want to change the young.

ANONYMOUS

WHEN YOU POP
OUT FOR MILK
AND COME HOME
WITH A NEW DOG
COLLAR AND
SOME PLANT POTS
THAT WERE ON
SPECIAL OFFER...
BUT NO MILK.

Don't let ageing get you down.
It's too hard to get back up.

JOHN WAGNER

WHEN YOU DECIDE IT'S
TIME TO PULL UP YOUR
SOCKS, AND REALIZE YOU
FORGOT TO PUT ANY ON.

> Long after wearing bifocals and hearing aids, we'll still be making love. We just won't know with whom.

JACK PAAR

" Early to rise and early to bed makes a man healthy, wealthy and dead.

JAMES THURBER "

"

Middle age is when your old classmates are so grey and wrinkled and bald they don't recognize you.

"

BENNETT CERF

WHEN CHILDREN START ASKING YOU WHAT LIFE WAS LIKE "IN THE OLDEN DAYS".

"

Here's God's cruel joke: by
the time a guy figures out how
women work, his penis doesn't.

ADAM CAROLLA "

WHEN YOU PHONE A
RELATIVE FROM ABROAD FOR
THEIR FULL ADDRESS, SO
YOU CAN SEND A POSTCARD
AND LET THEM KNOW HOW
YOU'RE GETTING ON.

WHEN YOU MENTION TO YOUR FRIEND BETTY THAT YOU MUST PHONE BETTY WHEN YOU GET THE CHANCE.

**Never look backwards or
you'll fall down the stairs.**

RUDYARD KIPLING

> The older we get, the
> better we used to be.

JOHN McENROE

WHEN YOU SUDDENLY
WONDER WHY THERE ARE
SO MANY CARS DRIVING
ON THE WRONG SIDE
OF THE ROAD TODAY.

You can't turn back
the clock but you can
wind it up again.

BONNIE PRUDDEN

WHEN YOU BECOME FRUSTRATED BY INSTRUCTIONS TO "PRESS ANY KEY" – WHY WOULD THEY TELL YOU TO DO THAT WHEN THERE'S NO "ANY" KEY ON YOUR KEYBOARD?

WHEN YOUR HAIR IS
FAR WHITER THAN
YOUR TEETH ARE.

"

Middle age is when
your age starts to show
around your middle.

BOB HOPE

"

66

Do I exercise? Well, I once
jogged to the ashtray.

WILL SELF

99

WHEN YOUR ENTHUSIASTIC EFFORTS TO CATCH THE ATTENTION OF A FRIEND IN THE STREET ARE MET WITH LOOKS OF INCREASING TERROR AS YOU DRAW NEARER AND EMBRACE A COMPLETE STRANGER.

WHEN THE STRAINED LOOKS ON THE FACES OF YOUR FRIENDS AND FAMILY TELL YOU THEY HAVE HEARD THIS STORY BEFORE. MANY TIMES.

My nan said, "What do you mean when you say the computer went down on you?"

JOSEPH LONGTHORNE

"

Youth is when you're allowed
to stay up late on New
Year's Eve. Middle age is
when you're forced to.

BILL VAUGHAN

"

Always pat children on
the head whenever you
meet them, just in case
they happen to be yours.

AUGUSTUS JOHN

In dog years, I'm dead.

ANONYMOUS

WHEN THE LOCAL CHARITY
SHOP IS VERY PLEASED TO
ACCEPT YOUR DONATION
OF BRAND-NEW CLOTHES,
STILL IN THEIR BAGS
FROM YESTERDAY'S
SHOPPING TRIP.

WHEN YOU
MISTAKE YOUR
ELECTRIC
BLANKET
KICKING IN FOR
A HOT FLUSH.

> True terror is to wake up
> one morning and discover
> that your high school class
> is running the country.

KURT VONNEGUT

WHEN YOU'RE
PLEASANTLY
SURPRISED
BY THE OFFER
TO "ACCEPT
COOKIES" ON A
NEW WEBSITE.

Middle age is having a choice
between two temptations and
choosing the one that'll get
you home earlier.

DAN BENNETT

"
I refuse to admit that I am more
than 52, even if that makes
my children illegitimate.

NANCY ASTOR
"

WHEN YOU REALIZE YOU CAN RE-READ THE SAME BOOK EVERY YEAR BECAUSE YOU WON'T REMEMBER ANY OF THE PLOT OR CHARACTERS FROM LAST TIME.

WHEN YOUR DENTIST SEEMS A BIT BAFFLED AS YOU START TO UNDRESS FOR YOUR YEARLY CHECK-UP.

"

Anyone can get old. All you have to do is live long enough.

GROUCHO MARX

"

There will always be death and taxes; however, death doesn't get worse every year.

ANONYMOUS

WHEN YOU FIND YOURSELF
WONDERING HOW IT'S
POSSIBLE TO HAVE A
HUNDRED CHANNELS ON
YOUR TV BUT NOTHING
WORTH WATCHING
ON ANY OF THEM.

WHEN A NEIGHBOUR REMARKS UPON HOW WELL YOUR RUBBER GLOVES COMPLEMENT YOUR EVENING DRESS.

"
Pushing 40? She's hanging
on for dear life.

IVY COMPTON-BURNETT "

I don't have any children, I have four middle-aged people.

DICK VAN DYKE

Growing old is like being increasingly penalized for a crime you haven't committed.

ANTHONY POWELL

"

The years between 50 and
70 are the hardest. You are
always asked to do things,
and yet you are not decrepit
enough to turn them down.

"

T. S. ELIOT

WHEN YOU KINDLY
OFFER A GUEST
FREE CHOICE
FROM YOUR BOWL
OF ORNAMENTAL
PLASTIC FRUIT.

WHEN YOU REQUEST A
TAXI PICK-UP FROM YOUR
ADDRESS OF 30 YEARS AGO.

Youth is the time of getting,
middle age of improving
and old age of spending.

ANNE BRADSTREET

WHEN YOU
REQUIRE A PEN
AND PAPER TO
ORDER A ROUND
OF DRINKS.

" An archaeologist is the best husband a woman can have: the older she gets, the more interested he is in her.

AGATHA CHRISTIE "

Memorial services are
the cocktail parties of
the geriatric set.

HAROLD MACMILLAN

WHEN MOST POLITICIANS
LOOK BARELY OLD ENOUGH
TO BUY A BOTTLE OF
WHISKY LET ALONE
RUN THE COUNTRY.

You know you're getting old when the candles cost more than the cake.

BOB HOPE

Senior Moment

WHEN YOU CAN'T
REMEMBER THE
LAST TIME YOU
HAD A SENIOR
MOMENT!

WHEN YOU FIND YOURSELF
ENJOYING A HEALTHY
MORNING BOWL OF
CRUNCHY CAT TREATS.

“

The past is the only dead
thing that smells sweet.

CYRIL CONNOLLY

WHEN YOU
ASK YOURSELF
IF THERE'S
ANYTHING
THAT MOBILE
PHONES CAN'T
DO NOWADAYS.

"

The first 100 years
are the hardest.

WILSON MIZNER

"

"

The first sign of maturity is
the discovery that the volume
knob also turns to the left.

"

JERRY M. WRIGHT

The three ages of man:
youth, middle age and
"my word you do look well".

JUNE WHITFIELD

WHEN YOU CALL YOUR PARTNER BY YOUR PET'S NAME, AND VICE VERSA.

Nice to be here? At my age
it's nice to be anywhere.

GEORGE BURNS

"

I don't feel old. I don't feel
anything till noon. That's
when it's time for my nap.

BOB HOPE

"

WHEN YOU
EVENTUALLY
MANAGE TO MAKE
IT TO THE TOP
OF THE LADDER
BEFORE IT DAWNS
ON YOU THAT
IT'S AGAINST THE
WRONG WALL.

I used to think I'd like less grey
hair. Now I'd like more of it.

RICHIE BENAUD

WHEN YOUR FRIEND
ARRIVES AT THE ALLOTMENT
AND ASKS HOW LONG IT
HAS TAKEN YOU TO WEED
AND HOE HIS PATCH.

WHEN YOU REACH
FOR A 5-IRON
ON THE GOLF
COURSE AND PULL
OUT YOUR NEW,
LIGHTWEIGHT
WALKING STICK.

At my age "getting lucky" means finding my car in the parking lot.

ANONYMOUS

The easiest way to diminish the appearance of wrinkles is to keep your glasses off when you look in the mirror.

JOAN RIVERS

As we grow older, our bodies get shorter and our anecdotes longer.

ROBERT QUILLEN

"

Everything slows down with age,
except the time it takes cake and
ice cream to reach your hips.

JOHN WAGNER

"

WHEN MOST OF YOUR INTERACTIONS WITH PEOPLE BEGIN, "AH, BUT BACK IN MY DAY…"

WHEN EVERY PARTY IS NOW A SURPRISE PARTY – INCLUDING THE ONES YOU HOST.

> You're getting old when the only thing you want for your birthday is not to be reminded of it.

ANONYMOUS

WHEN YOU START
SPEEDING ON
THE MOTORWAY
SO YOU DON'T
FORGET WHERE
YOU WERE GOING.

Each year it grows harder to make ends meet – the ends I refer to are hands and feet.

RICHARD ARMOUR

"

Almost all of my middle-aged
and elderly acquaintances,
including me, feel about 25,
unless we haven't had our coffee,
in which case we feel 107.

MARTHA BECK

"

WHEN SOMEONE ASKS YOU HOW LARGE YOUR CARBON FOOTPRINT IS, AND YOU REPLY, "I'M SO SORRY, I THOUGHT I WIPED MY FEET AS I CAME IN!"

" I believe in loyalty. When a
woman reaches a certain age she
likes, she should stick with it.

EVA GABOR

"

WHEN YOU SPEND THE AFTERNOON GOING THROUGH OLD PHOTO ALBUMS, BUT CAN'T REMEMBER WHO ANY OF THE PEOPLE ARE IN THE PICTURES.

WHEN YOU LOOK FORWARD
TO TAKING ASPIRIN
BECAUSE THEY TASTE
NICE, ONLY TO DISCOVER
IT'S A PACKET OF MINTS.

" Old age and treachery will always beat youth and exuberance. **"**

DAVID MAMET

**Fun is like life insurance;
the older you get,
the more it costs.**

KIN HUBBARD

You can judge your age by
the amount of pain you
feel when you come in
contact with a new idea.

PEARL S. BUCK

I don't need you to remind
me of my age. I have a
bladder to do that for me.

STEPHEN FRY

WHEN AFTER
QUEUING FOR
HALF AN HOUR
TO BUY STAMPS
IN THE POST
OFFICE, YOU
FORGET TO STICK
THEM ON ANY OF
YOUR LETTERS.

WHEN YOU REALIZE THAT
MOST OF YOUR JOINTS
HAVE BEEN PUT THERE
BY SURGICAL TEAMS.

Wisdom doesn't necessarily come with age. Sometimes age just shows up all by itself.

TOM WILSON

WHEN YOU'RE NOT
SURE WHETHER
YOU WERE
GETTING IN OR
OUT OF THE BATH.

For all the advances in
medicine, there is still no cure
for the common birthday.

JOHN GLENN

" Youth is a wonderful thing.
What a crime to waste
it on children.

GEORGE BERNARD SHAW "

WHEN YOU GO TO PAY
FOR SOME FUEL AND THE
PRICE IS SO HIGH YOU
THINK THEY MUST BE
SELLING YOU A NEW CAR.

Why is a birthday cake the only food you can blow on and spit on and everybody rushes to get a piece?

BOBBY KELTON

WHEN YOUR
SCHOOL REUNION
SEEMS LIKE A
ROOM FULL OF
STRANGERS
WITH VAGUELY
FAMILIAR NAMES.

WHEN TODAY'S NEWSPAPER SEEMS STRANGELY FAMILIAR – THEY'VE EVEN REPEATED YESTERDAY'S FRONT PAGE HEADLINE!

I am getting to an age
when I can only enjoy the
last sport left. It is called
hunting for your spectacles.

EDWARD GREY

WHEN YOU STOP TO ADMIRE THE SNOWY HILLS IN VIEW OF YOUR HOUSE AND DISCOVER (AFTER FIVE YEARS OF LIVING THERE) THAT THEY ARE CHALK CLIFFS.

The elderly don't drive that badly; they're just the only ones with time to do the speed limit.

JASON LOVE

" Beautiful young people are accidents of nature, but beautiful old people are works of art.

ELEANOR ROOSEVELT

WHEN YOU WONDER WHY
YOUR COAT APPEARS TO
HAVE A KINK IN IT WHEN
YOU CATCH SIGHT OF
YOUR REFLECTION IN A
SHOP WINDOW, AND LATER
FIND THAT THE COAT
HANGER IS STILL INSIDE.

Whenever a man's friends begin
to compliment him about looking
young, he may be sure that
they think he is growing old.

WASHINGTON IRVING

Middle age is when your broad mind and narrow waist begin to change places.

E. JOSEPH COSSMAN

WHEN YOU
RESORT TO
OPENING A
CHILD-PROOF
LID WITH A
MALLET.

Old people are fond of giving good advice; it consoles them for no longer being capable of setting a bad example.

FRANÇOIS DE LA
ROCHEFOUCAULD

You know you're old if they have discontinued your blood type.

PHYLLIS DILLER

WHEN YOU HAVE A
MOMENT OF PANIC AND
FRANTICALLY CHECK YOUR
TRAIN TICKET TO REMIND
YOU WHERE YOU'RE MEANT
TO BE TRAVELLING TO.

To me, old age is always 15 years older than I am.

BERNARD BARUCH

WHEN YOU FIND
VEGETABLE
PEELINGS IN THE
CLOTHES BASKET,
AND SUDDENLY
UNDERSTAND
WHY THE WASTE
DISPOSAL UNIT
IS BLOCKED.

The secret to staying young
is to live honestly, eat slowly
and lie about your age.

LUCILLE BALL

Some people are old when they're 18 and some people are young when they're 90.

YOKO ONO

WHEN YOU GO UPSTAIRS
TO GET SOMETHING,
FORGET WHAT IT WAS, AND
COME DOWNSTAIRS WITH
SOMETHING ELSE YOU
DIDN'T KNOW YOU NEEDED.

"

Birthdays are good for
you. Statistics show that
the people who have the
most live the longest.

LARRY LORENZONI

Sure I'm for helping the elderly. I'm going to be old myself someday.

LILLIAN GORDY CARTER

“ Age is an issue of mind
over matter. If you don’t
mind, it doesn’t matter.

MARK TWAIN

If you're interested in finding out more about our books, find us on Facebook at **Summersdale Publishers** and follow us on Twitter at **@Summersdale**.

www.summersdale.com